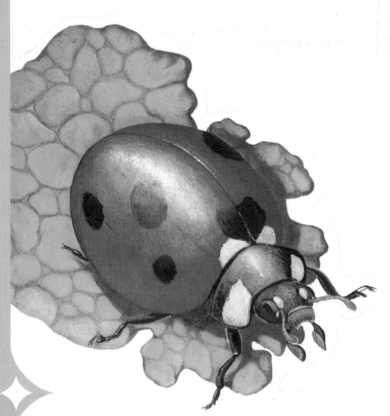

INTRODUCTION

---◆---

Our planet is teeming with billions of amazing insects. From spiders and beetles to bees and dragonflies, wherever you are in the world, you're never far from a critter of some kind. With more than one million insect species worldwide, the variety of colors, patterns, shapes, and behavior is fascinating and seemingly never-ending.

→ GO TO PAGE 17 FOR THE LADYBUG

→ GO TO PAGE 39 FOR THE ASSASSIN BUG

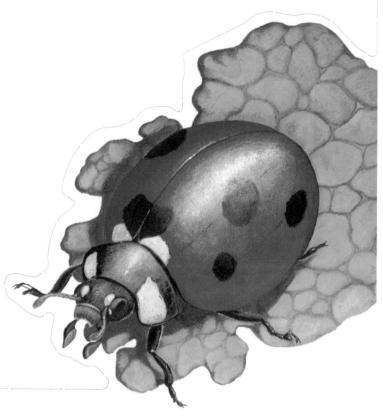

There are bugs that fly, run fast, or leap great distances, and there are those that can only crawl along slowly. There are bugs that shout out a rainbow of colors, and there are those that blend in quietly with their habitat. There are bugs that bite with powerful, sawlike jaws, and there are those that have no mouth at all. There are bugs with spikes or a venomous sting, or that disguise themselves as bigger, more dangerous creatures than they are—all clever defenses to keep enemies at bay.

Read on to discover 29 of these weird and wonderful insects. You'll learn awesome facts to impress your family and friends with, and have fun creating a colorful bug parade.

GO TO PAGE 59 FOR THE FIREFLY

ULTIMATE AERIAL KILLER!

BLUE-SPOTTED HAWKER *Adversaeschna brevistyla*

No flying insects are as fast—or as powerful —as these fierce hunters. Some kinds of dragonfly can reach speeds of more than 50 feet a second! A dragonfly uses its huge eyes to pick out its unsuspecting prey. Then it hones in on the tiny insect like a guided missile. It uses its dangling legs like a spiky claw to scoop up its target. Once the insect is caught in the dragonfly's leggy cage, or basket, the dragonfly bites it to hold it in place. Although they are fierce hunters, dragonflies don't usually sting or bite people, and they don't carry diseases or germs.

SIZE: 3.5 inch wingspan

FOOD: small flying insects such as gnats, moths, and flies

LIFESPAN: up to 7 years (most as a young nymph)

CONSERVATION STATUS: not threatened

DANGER LEVEL: low—they can draw blood with a bite if you pick them up

The blue-spotted hawker eats its small victims on the wing—a delicious in-flight snack! If its prey is larger, the dragonfly zips back to a perch for a "sit down" meal.

HABITAT

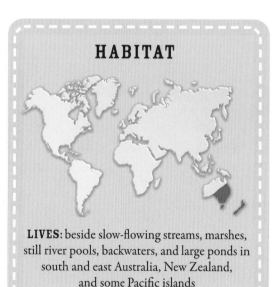

LIVES: beside slow-flowing streams, marshes, still river pools, backwaters, and large ponds in south and east Australia, New Zealand, and some Pacific islands

DID YOU KNOW ...?

❓ Dragonflies have four wings, which they flap in alternate pairs, first the front pair and then the rear. They can fly forward, up, down, and sideways.

❓ The blue-spotted hawker has very distinctive colors and markings. There are two large blue spots on its head that give it its name, as well as a "cat face" on its back near the base of its wings.

❓ The female blue-spotted hawker lays her eggs in plant tissue or sometimes in soft mud.

TRAP-SETTER

TRAPDOOR SPIDER *Liphistius* and more

—— ◆ ——

The trapdoor spider is named after its cleverly disguised burrow, and there are about 50 species living in the world today. One species, the Kanthan cave trapdoor spider, may look scary with its sharp fangs, but it is generally harmless to humans. It spends most of its time underground waiting for its victims to trip over the silky threads it spins around the entrance to its home. Made from mud and moss, the camouflaged trapdoor is easy to miss. When the spider senses a silk thread being triggered, it zips out of its secret hatch and snatches the passing prey.

 SIZE: 0.9–1.5 inches long

 FOOD: mice, insects, frogs and small fish, baby birds, and snakes

 LIFESPAN: 5–20 years

 CONSERVATION STATUS: *Liphistius kanthan* is critically endangered

 DANGER LEVEL: low—if attacked, this spider may give you a painful bite

The trapdoor spider doesn't stray far from home, preferring to drag victims back to its underground silk-lined den.

HABITAT

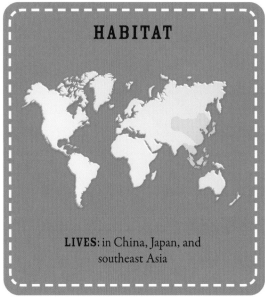

LIVES: in China, Japan, and southeast Asia

DID YOU KNOW ...?

❓ Not all trapdoor spiders actually build a door, but they all hide at the entrance to their homes waiting to catch a tasty dinner. And they have eight eyes . . . all the better to spot their meals!

❓ The now critically endangered *Liphistius kanthan* lives in just one cave in Malaysia.

❓ *Liphistius kanthan* spins six to eight tripwire threads around its front door. It puts a leg on each thread and waits for prey.

FLOWER POWER!

BUMBLEBEE *Bombus*

The bumblebee is a sociable insect that lives in colonies of up to 200. All the bees apart from the queen die off after one season. The queen hibernates underground in winter, emerging in spring to search for a spot to nest and lay her eggs. Bumblebees produce little honey, but they pollinate many flowers and fruit trees. Their buzzing vibrations cause flowers to release pollen, which then sticks to the bees and is passed from one flower to another as the bees visit them. The bees comb the pollen stuck to their fur into special "baskets" on their hind legs and carry it back to the nest.

 SIZE: up to 0.5 inches long

 FOOD: pollen and nectar

 LIFESPAN: 28 days

 CONSERVATION STATUS: not threatened

 DANGER LEVEL: low—if attacked, bumblebees will give a sharp sting but, unless you're allergic, you'll feel fine again soon

The gentle bumblebee can sting more than once, but usually only stings if it is threatened.

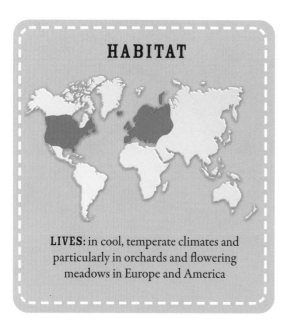

HABITAT

LIVES: in cool, temperate climates and particularly in orchards and flowering meadows in Europe and America

DID YOU KNOW ...?

❓ There are over 260 species of bumblebee in the world today.

❓ A bumblebee can beat its wings more than 130 times per second. However, its hypnotic buzz isn't caused by the rapid beating of its wings, but by its vibrating flight muscles!

❓ These bees build their waxy nest in an underground hole, often one left behind by a small burrowing animal, such as a mouse.

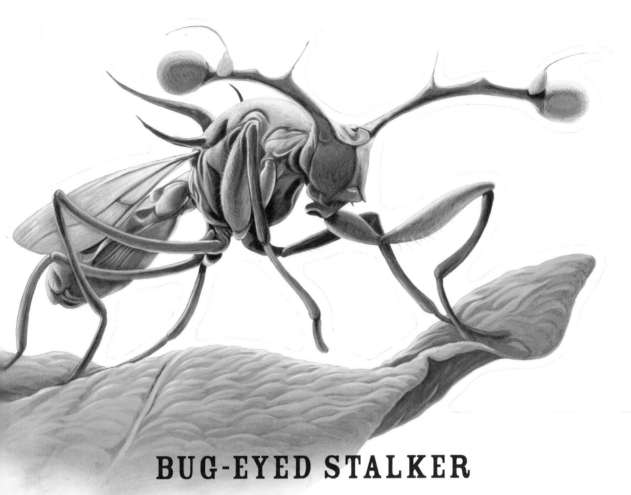

BUG-EYED STALKER

STALK-EYED FLY *Diopsidae*

This little fly is distinctive because its two red eyes are out on stalks! Each eyestalk can be up to 0.3 inches long, which is sometimes longer than the bug's entire body. These flies are plant eaters so they don't need improved vision from their eyestalks for hunting. But the females seem to prefer males with longer eyestalks, and the males love to show off their stalks by stretching them out sideways as far as they possibly can. They battle with other long-stalked males, much like deer locking antlers. The champion gets to mate with the lady (or ladies!) that turn up to watch.

 SIZE: 0.15–0.4 inches long

 FOOD: bacteria, fungi, and rotting vegetation

 LIFESPAN: unknown

 CONSERVATION STATUS: not threatened

 DANGER LEVEL: none

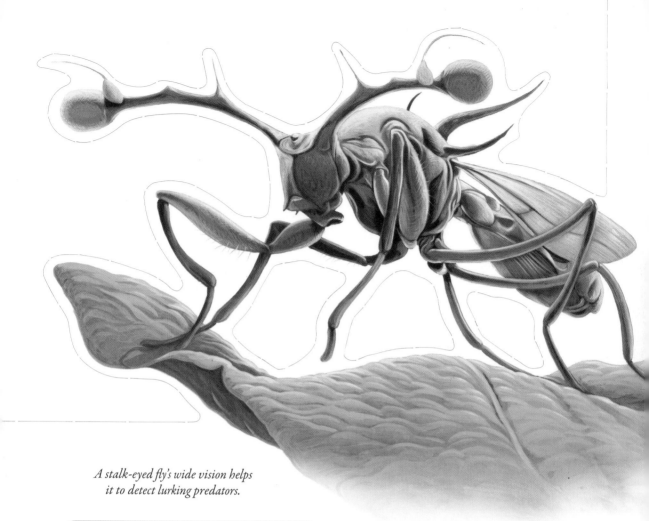

*A stalk-eyed fly's wide vision helps
it to detect lurking predators.*

HABITAT

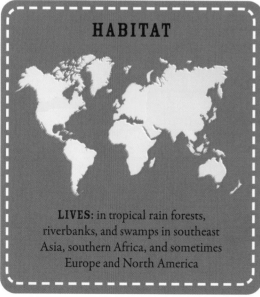

LIVES: in tropical rain forests,
riverbanks, and swamps in southeast
Asia, southern Africa, and sometimes
Europe and North America

DID YOU KNOW...?

❓ There are about 100 species of stalk-eyed
fly. These flies have antennae on their eyestalks
as well as their eyes.

❓ The newborn nymphs pump air into each
of their soft, transparent eyestalks to make
them longer.

❓ The male's eyestalks are usually longer than
the female's. The longer stalks make it more
difficult to fly efficiently—which isn't so
handy for escaping enemies in a hurry.

HEAVYWEIGHT HOPPER

GIANT WETA *Deinacrida*

- - - - ◆ - - - -

The giant weta is the heaviest insect in the world. Adults can weigh up to 0.7 ounces (20 grams) and grow almost three inches long—the same length as a mouse! This ancient relative of the grasshopper has roamed New Zealand for about 190 million years. Its exoskeleton (a skeleton on the outside of the body) and the thorny spikes on its hind legs help defend this slow-moving, wingless bug from predators. In addition to its awesome insect armor, the giant weta can scare off enemies with a loud rasping sound, made by rubbing its leg spines across its abdomen.

SIZE: 2.9 inch-long body

FOOD: leaves and vegetation

LIFESPAN: 2 years

CONSERVATION STATUS: endangered

DANGER LEVEL: low—although a few species bite, none are poisonous

Hundreds of years ago, human settlers introduced cats and rats to New Zealand. Sadly, since then, these animals have hunted the weta to the verge of extinction.

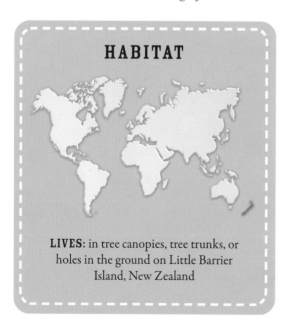

HABITAT

LIVES: in tree canopies, tree trunks, or holes in the ground on Little Barrier Island, New Zealand

DID YOU KNOW ... ?

❓ A female giant weta lays 200 to 300 eggs during her adult life. Her long ovipositor (needlelike egg-laying tube) can deposit eggs up to two inches underground. It takes about 10 months for the eggs to hatch.

❓ The nymph sheds its exoskeleton 10 times before reaching adulthood.

❓ The name *weta* comes from the Maori *wetapunga*, meaning "god of ugly things."

NOW YOU SEE ME!

SPINY FLOWER MANTIS *Pseudocreobotra wahlbergi*

This colorful mantis has a distinctive bright-yellow eyespot on each of its forewings. When threatened, it spreads its arms and wings and rears up on its hind legs to make itself look bigger and scarier. The spiny flower mantis can also disguise itself as a pretty flower. Its spines may look vicious, but they help it blend in with the African plants where it lives. To catch prey, this well-camouflaged critter sits very still on a flower and waits. As soon as a bug flies by, the mantis catches it in midair with lightning speed.

SIZE: up to 2 inches long

FOOD: small insects, such as moths and flies

LIFESPAN: 6 months to 1 year

CONSERVATION STATUS: not threatened

DANGER LEVEL: none

*The spiny flower mantis has
a spiky white-and-orange body with green
stripes, and green-and-yellow forewings.*

HABITAT

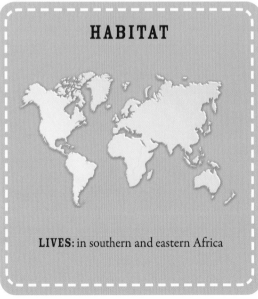

LIVES: in southern and eastern Africa

DID YOU KNOW ...?

❓ Most mantises are cannibals, which means they eat each other. Often the female gobbles up the male once they've finished mating ... charming!

❓ Just before winter, the female creates a foamy protective egg case, called an ootheca, for around 55 eggs.

❓ The tiny black hatchlings, called nymphs, look like miniature adults. They are very hungry when they first hatch and may try to eat one another.

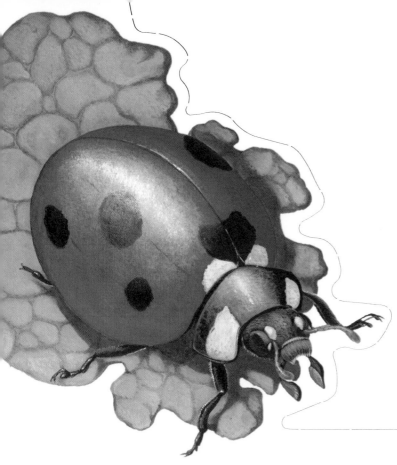

BRIGHT SPOTTY DEFENDER

LADYBUG *Coccinellidae*

— — — ◆ — — —

All around the world, ladybugs are seen as symbols of love, joy, and happiness. They are actually a type of beetle. Other common names include lady beetle and ladybird. There are about 5,000 species of ladybug worldwide, and although most commonly have red, orange, or yellow bodies with black spots, there are many other variations of colors and patterns. Ladybugs' bright colors warn predators to stay away but if threatened, these bright little beetles ooze a foul-tasting fluid from their leg joints to ward off attack.

 SIZE: 0.07–0.3 inches long

 FOOD: small plant-eating insects, such as aphids and greenfly

 LIFESPAN: about 2 years

 CONSERVATION STATUS: not threatened

 DANGER LEVEL: low—harmless to humans and their pets but not other insects

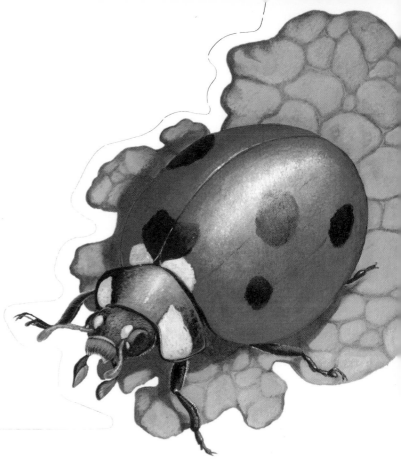

The seven-spotted ladybug (Coccinella septempunctata) is the most common species throughout Europe. It has two shiny, red protective wing cases, each with three black spots; the seventh spot spans both wing cases.

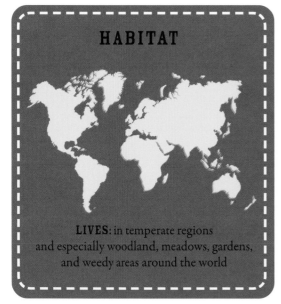

HABITAT

LIVES: in temperate regions and especially woodland, meadows, gardens, and weedy areas around the world

DID YOU KNOW ...?

❓ Around the world, ladybugs are seen as signs of good luck. Some people say that if a ladybug lands on you, the number of spots on its back will bring you that many months of good luck. Others say that the brighter the ladybug, the more luck it will bring you.

❓ A ladybug flaps its wings about 85 times a second when in flight.

❓ Some ladybugs don't have any spots on their back, and *Paramysia oblonguttata* has stripes instead of spots!

FIERCE AND DEADLY!

ASIAN GIANT HORNET *Vespa mandarinia*

- - - ◆ - - -

The Asian giant hornet is the fiercest hornet in the world. A swarm of 20 to 30 hornets can destroy a 30,000-strong bee colony in just a few hours. It is the biggest of all the wasps and bees, with a body easily as big as your thumb! Its stinger is about 0.2 inches long—that's about the same size as the sharp part of a drawing pin. When it stings a person, it feels like a small, hot nail is being hammered through their skin! Like all insects, however, the giant hornet does not deliberately look for people to harm. If someone is stung, the hornet is usually acting in self-defense.

 SIZE: 2-inch-long body, 3 inch wingspan

 FOOD: other insects, like wasps and bees

 LIFESPAN: 1–2 years for queen, 2–3 months for worker

 CONSERVATION STATUS: not threatened

 DANGER LEVEL: high—they injure and kill people every year

The Asian giant hornet injects its prey with a venom made from eight different chemicals before slicing it up!

HABITAT

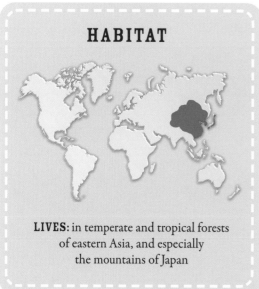

LIVES: in temperate and tropical forests of eastern Asia, and especially the mountains of Japan

DID YOU KNOW ...?

❓ One Asian giant hornet can kill around 40 honeybees in less than a minute!

❓ The Asian giant hornet can travel at speeds of up to 25 miles per hour, over a distance of 60 miles, to catch its prey.

❓ Like bees, Asian giant hornets live in colonies that are made up of workers, drones, and a queen. The workers collect food, take care of the young, and protect the nest. The drones fertilize the queen, and the queen lays eggs and establishes a new colony every year.

MASTER OF THE AIR

ATLAS MOTH *Attacus atlas*

One of the biggest insects on Earth, this mega moth has a wingspan bigger than the open hand of an average adult human. Unfortunately, the life of this stunning, nocturnal creature is fleeting; it has no mouth, so it cannot eat. Instead, it survives on the energy it stored during its time as a very hungry caterpillar. The caterpillars grow up to 4.7 inches long, and they eat citrus fruit and cinnamon leaves. The adult moth spends its short life flying around in search of a mate. Once breeding occurs and the females lay their eggs, the atlas moths die.

SIZE: up to 10.6 inch wingspan

FOOD: none

LIFESPAN: 1–2 weeks

CONSERVATION STATUS: not threatened

DANGER LEVEL: none

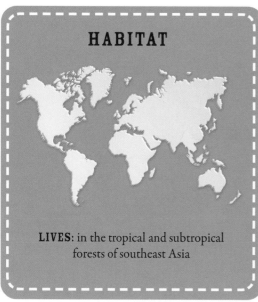

The majestic atlas moth emerges from its cocoon after four weeks, then flies off in search of a mate.

HABITAT

LIVES: in the tropical and subtropical forests of southeast Asia

DID YOU KNOW...?

❓ In Taiwan, the strong silk cocoons of the atlas moth are sometimes used as purses.

❓ The atlas moth caterpillar defends itself from predators by spraying a foul-smelling substance up to a distance of 20 inches.

❓ The markings on the wing tips of the atlas moth resemble snake heads. When threatened, the moth falls to the ground and slowly flaps its wings to resemble the moving head and neck of a cobra—enough to ward off most would-be predators.

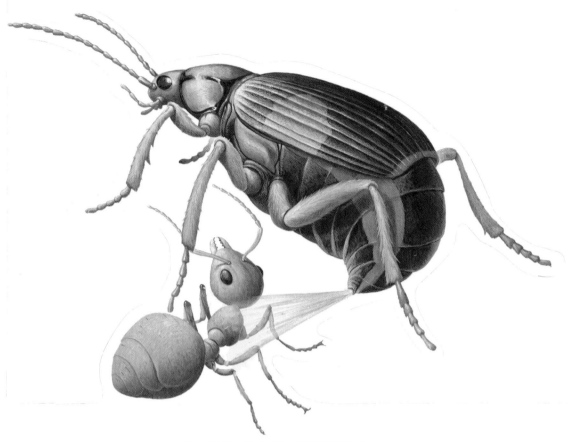

BULL'S EYE!

BOMBARDIER BEETLE *Brachinus, Stenaptinus,* and more

More than 500 species of bombardier beetle exist worldwide. You can identify one by its dark blue, green, or black shelllike body and orange head. This bug needs time to prepare for flight, so instead of trying to escape, it has a nasty surprise in its butt (yes, its butt) for any enemy that tries to attack! It fires a stinking, hot concoction of gas and chemicals out of its rear end. It can also rotate its flexible abdomen up to 270 degrees, allowing it to fire at enemies with amazing accuracy. It's this effective defensive weapon that gives the bombardier its name.

 SIZE: 1 inches long

 FOOD: small insects, spiders and worms

 LIFESPAN: 2–3 years

 CONSERVATION STATUS: not threatened

 DANGER LEVEL: moderate— a defensive explosion can cause a slight burn that stains your skin

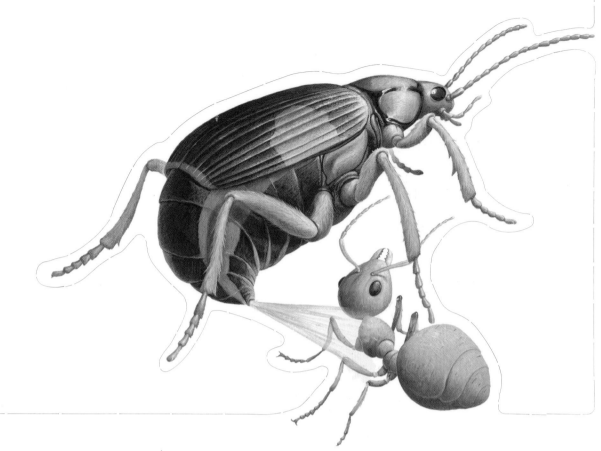

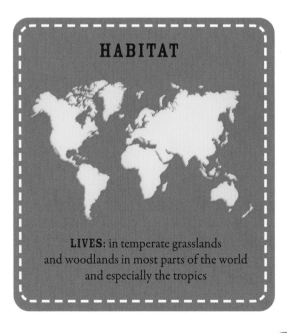

A bombardier beetle shoots its toxic spray directly at an attacking ant.

HABITAT

LIVES: in temperate grasslands and woodlands in most parts of the world and especially the tropics

DID YOU KNOW ... ?

❓ The bombardier beetle was once known as the shooting fly beetle because of the mix of gas and chemicals that it fires from its rear end.

❓ The bombardier beetle can squirt its toxic potion up to a distance of 7.8 inches. When ejected, the chemicals combine to create a burning, hot spray that makes a popping sound when it hits its target.

❓ The beetle's defensive chemicals are stored in two separate abdominal chambers. If they weren't separated, the beetle would die.

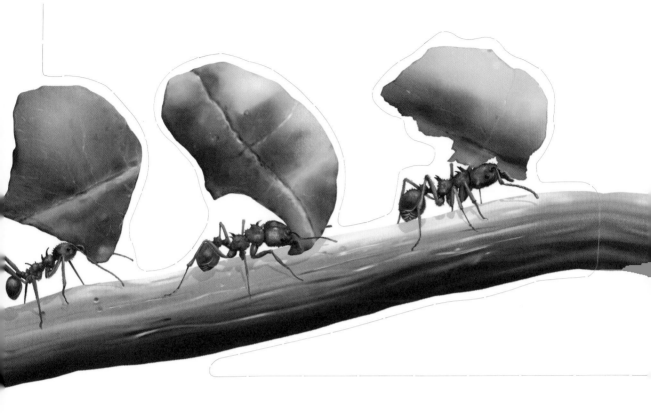

FUNGUS FARMERS

LEAFCUTTER ANT *Atta and Acromyrmex*

- - - ◆ - - -

There are more than 40 species of leafcutter ant worldwide. They live in underground colonies where each ant has a specific duty. Worker ants use their sharp, powerful jaws for cutting up leaves to carry back to their nest. This kind of work wears down the ants' jaws, so they have to change jobs after a while. They march like an army in a procession up to 98 feet long. They don't actually eat the leaves that they collect. Instead, they chew them up and use them to grow a fungus found only in leafcutter ant nests. This special fungus becomes the leafcutter ants' food.

 SIZE: 0.7 inches long (worker), 0.8 inches long (queen)

 FOOD: leaves and fungus

 LIFESPAN: 1–2 years (worker), 10–15 years (queen)

 CONSERVATION STATUS: not threatened

 DANGER LEVEL: moderate—the leafcutter ant can deliver a nasty cut, and it normally has an army behind it

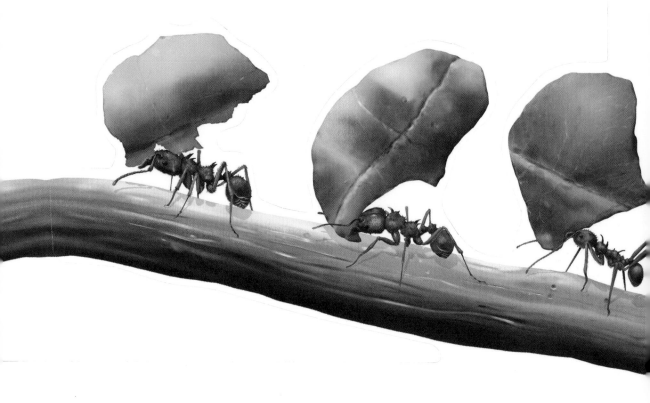

Leafcutter ants can carry more than 50 times their own body weight with their powerful jaws.

HABITAT

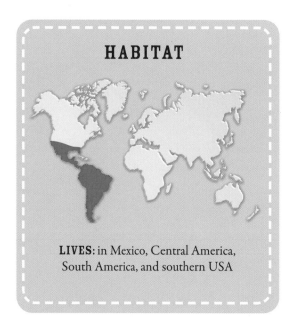

LIVES: in Mexico, Central America, South America, and southern USA

DID YOU KNOW ... ?

❓ A leafcutter nest can contain 10 million ants, all living underground in an enormous network of tunnels and chambers.

❓ The ants each have different jobs. Some are soldiers, others are workers, and a few are minims. Minims ride on the cut leaves and swipe off any parasites to prevent disease entering the nest.

❓ A colony of foraging worker ants can strip a tree of its leaves in under 24 hours.

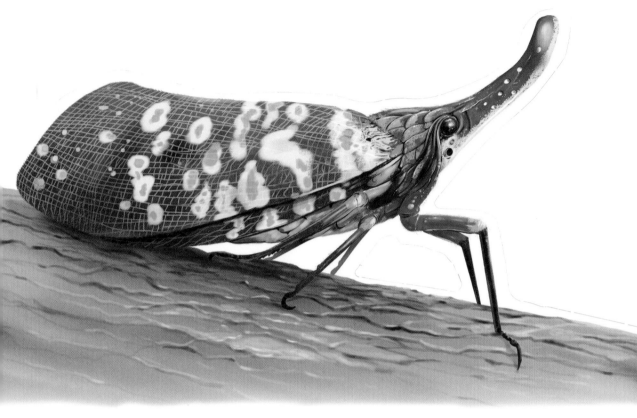

LEADING THE WAY!

LANTERN BUG *Pyrops candelaria* and others

◆

Lantern bugs come in many vibrant colors and all sorts of patterns, although some are more muted, preferring to blend in with their leafy surroundings than stand out from the crowd. This curious little beastie has a long, curved snout, called a rostrum, which is half as long as its entire body. It uses this strawlike nozzle to suck up flower nectar or tree sap and to scare away enemies. Although it was once believed that their colorful snouts could glow in the dark, lantern bugs don't actually light up. Because of its long nose, this bug has even been nicknamed Pinocchio!

SIZE: 2-inch-long body, up to 3 inch wingspan

FOOD: fruit, flower nectar, and tree sap

LIFESPAN: unknown

CONSERVATION STATUS: not threatened

DANGER LEVEL: none

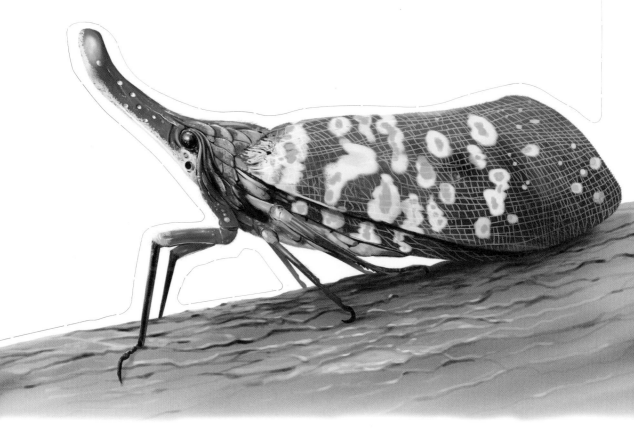

The red-nosed Pyrops candelaria *lives throughout southeast Asia and is a big fan of the sweet sap from lychee trees.*

HABITAT

LIVES: in the tropical forests of Vietnam, Laos, Thailand, Hong Kong, and other parts of southeast Asia

DID YOU KNOW...?

❓ Lantern bugs spend most of their life on the same tree. The female lays eggs on the host plant, and the baby nymphs hatch and mature close to the adults.

❓ The snakeheaded lantern bug has a snout shaped like the head of a snake complete with two false eyes. Some say the snout resembles a peanut.

❓ Some Amazonian legends say that a bite from a lantern bug can be deadly.

SKULL-FACED HONEY THIEF

DEATH'S-HEAD HAWKMOTH *Acherontia*

The death's-head hawkmoth gets its name from the unique human skull marking on the back of its thorax (the area between the head and the abdomen). This huge moth is the size of a bat, but although it looks scary, it isn't aggressive. If threatened, it will make a high-pitched squeak. The noise also acts as a disguise when it breaks into beehives to steal honey because it sounds like a queen bee. The moth even releases a bee-like scent to help it blend in with the colony. It's hardly surprising, then, that these moths are nicknamed bee-robbers.

 SIZE: 2.3 inch-long body, 5 inch wingspan

 FOOD: honey, tree sap, and rotting fruit

 LIFESPAN: up to 6 weeks

 CONSERVATION STATUS: not threatened

 DANGER LEVEL: none—scary to look at, but completely harmless

The death-head's forewings are mottled brown to provide camouflage when it rests on tree trunks during the day.

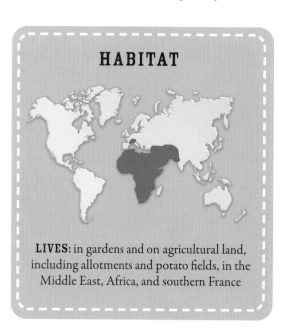

HABITAT

LIVES: in gardens and on agricultural land, including allotments and potato fields, in the Middle East, Africa, and southern France

DID YOU KNOW ...?

❓ The death's-head moth was once thought to be an omen of death because of its skull-like marking.

❓ The caterpillars can be brown, yellow, or green and grow up to five inches long. If threatened, they will try to bite.

❓ The moth makes a squeaking sound by blowing air out through its proboscis (tongue) across a vibrating structure, sismilar to playing a saxophone.

LONG-NECKED LEAF-EATER

GIRAFFE WEEVIL *Trachelophorus giraffa*

❖

No prizes for guessing how this bug got its name! The necks of the male of the species are two or even three times longer than those of the female. The males use these extraordinarily long necks to compete with each other for a female mate. Once mating takes place, the female uses her shorter neck to roll a leaf into a tube nest for a single egg. When the nest is complete, she snips the leaf from the plant so it falls to the forest floor, where it sits until the egg is ready to hatch. The hatchling will feed on the leaf for the first few days of its life.

SIZE: up to 1 inch-long body

FOOD: the leaves of the giraffe beetle tree

LIFESPAN: unknown

CONSERVATION STATUS: not threatened

DANGER LEVEL: none—these gentle bugs cannot bite or sting

The giraffe weevil has a bright red back and a long, shiny black neck and legs.

HABITAT

LIVES: in Madagascar

DID YOU KNOW ...?

❷ This remarkable bug was only discovered in 2008. It has no predators, although small insects may prey on its eggs.

❷ Although giraffe weevils can fly, they rarely stray far from the trees that they spend most of their adult lives on.

❷ During a battle for mating rights, the female waits patiently for a winner, sometimes even acting as a referee.

GREEDIEST GRUB!

LOCUST *Acrididae*

------- ◆ -------

A solitary locust doesn't cause anyone much harm, but billions of hungry swarming locusts are no laughing matter. Migratory locusts are one of the most destructive critters on Earth. When a swarm lands, it can easily cover up to 620 square miles of land and devour everything in sight, from crops to laundry on a clothesline! If swarming locusts find their way indoors, they'll happily munch through furniture, too! Locusts have such powerful jaws that the noise of a feasting swarm can be heard for miles around. One locust can eat its own body weight every day!

 SIZE: up to 2 inch-long body

 FOOD: fruit, vegetables, leaves, and grains

 LIFESPAN: a few months

 CONSERVATION STATUS: not threatened

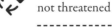 **DANGER LEVEL:** high—when they swarm together, they can wipe out crops, causing poverty and hunger

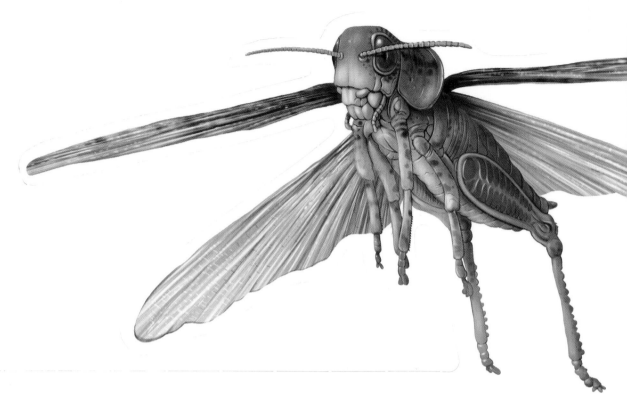

*The migratory locust has colorless wings
and a green, yellow, brown, or gray body.*

HABITAT

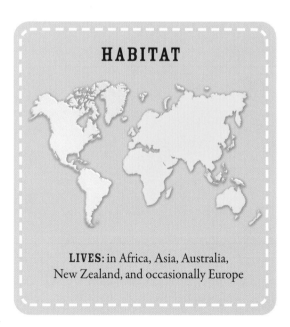

LIVES: in Africa, Asia, Australia,
New Zealand, and occasionally Europe

DID YOU KNOW ...?

❓ Locusts usually fly with the wind and
can travel at speeds of up to 12.5 miles
per hour. A swarm can travel up to 80 miles
per day.

❓ A locust can leap 27.5 inches, That's the
equivalent of a human achieving a 59-foot-
long jump.

❓ Female locusts lay one to three egg pods, each
containing 60–80 eggs. These eggs are light
brown and 2.8–3.2 inches long. Heavy rains are
the signal for eggs to hatch.

SUPER SURVIVOR!

AMERICAN COCKROACH *Periplaneta americana*

- - - - ◆ - - - -

Hardy cockroaches are older than the dinosaurs—they've been roaming Earth for more than 300 million years. There are more than 4,000 cockroach species worldwide, and the American cockroach is the second-most widespread one, after the German cockroach. The American roach isn't actually a native of North America, but was probably transported on ships from Africa back in the 17th century. It is often seen as a pest because it invades homes and businesses and can spread germs, contaminate food, and cause allergies.

 SIZE: 0.5–2 inch-long body

 FOOD: plants, insects, and almost anything else available

 LIFESPAN: about 1 year

 CONSERVATION STATUS: not threatened

 DANGER LEVEL: low—these bugs can spread disease by leaving poop on your food.

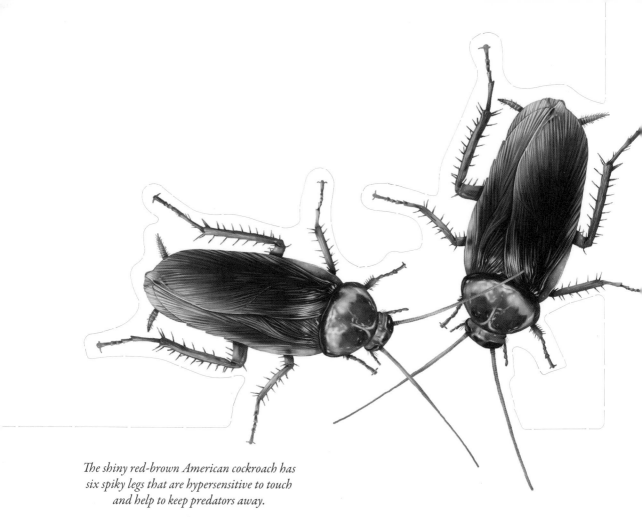

The shiny red-brown American cockroach has six spiky legs that are hypersensitive to touch and help to keep predators away.

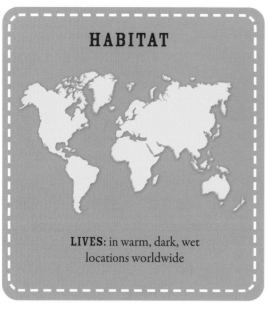

HABITAT

LIVES: in warm, dark, wet locations worldwide

DID YOU KNOW ...?

❓ A cockroach can stay alive for one week with its head missing! It doesn't need a mouth to breathe because it takes in oxygen through holes in its body. It can live for a month without food!

❓ A one-day-old baby roach can run fast enough to keep up with its parents.

❓ The biggest cockroach species in the world lives in South America. It grows up to six inches long with a wingspan of about 12 inches.

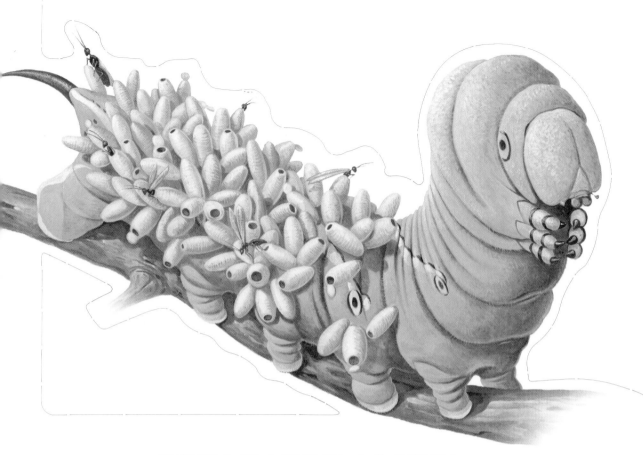

EEK! EATEN ALIVE!

BRACONID WASP LARVAE *Cotesia spp*

––––◆––––

To lay her eggs, the female braconid wasp uses an ovipositor—a long needlelike organ—to inject eggs into an unsuspecting host. Victims are commonly the hornworm caterpillar, but may also include aphids, flies, beetles, moths, butterflies, and other wasps. When a larva hatches, it slowly feasts on its host's insides, while cleverly avoiding any vital organs so the host stays alive long enough for the larva to reach adulthood. Once fully grown, the larva gnaws its way out of the host's body, spins itself a silk cocoon and within a short time emerges as a little adult wasp.

SIZE: up to 0.7 inches long

FOOD: aphids, flies, grasshoppers, bees, nectar, and tree sap

LIFESPAN: unknown

CONSERVATION STATUS: not threatened

DANGER LEVEL: none—to humans

Mature braconid larvae release a paralyzing chemical to keep the caterpillar still while they chew their way through to the outside world with their sharp teeth.

HABITAT

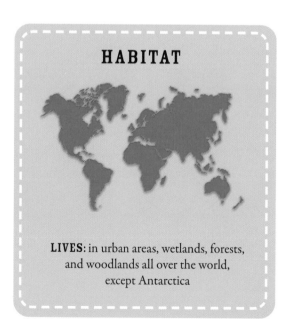

LIVES: in urban areas, wetlands, forests, and woodlands all over the world, except Antarctica

DID YOU KNOW ...?

❓ Around 17,000 species of braconid wasp have been found buzzing around the planet, and there are more to be discovered!

❓ Braconid wasps are usually black or brown in color, not bright yellow like typical wasps.

❓ A female braconid wasp can lay up to 200 eggs a day.

DEADLY DISGUISER

ASSASSIN BUG *Reduviidae*

- - - ◆ - - -

This fierce killing machine attacks and paralyzes its prey within seconds. It stabs its victim with its strong, sharp beak and injects a paralyzing poison that turns the victim's insides to liquid. The assassin bug sucks up its juicy dinner and then tosses the dead insect onto its back, along with any other insect corpses it collects along the way. This gruesome behavior provides effective camouflage and protective armor against enemies—which is useful since the assassin bug can't run too fast and isn't very good at flying.

 SIZE: 0.2–1.5 inch-long body

 FOOD: different insects according to species

 LIFESPAN: 6–12 months

 CONSERVATION STATUS: not threatened

 DANGER LEVEL: low—if picked up, this bug may give a painful bite but it isn't deadly

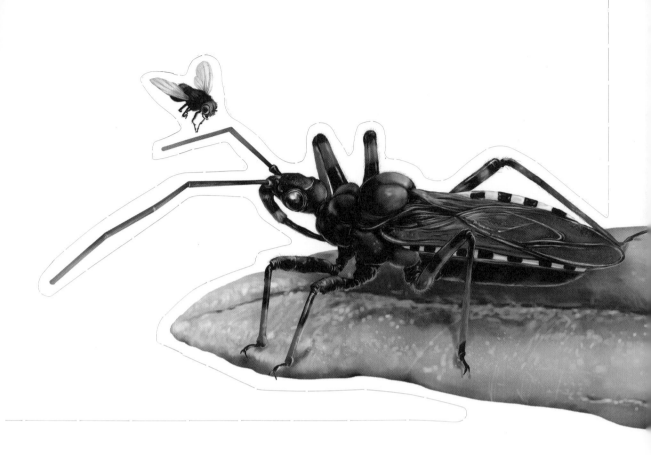

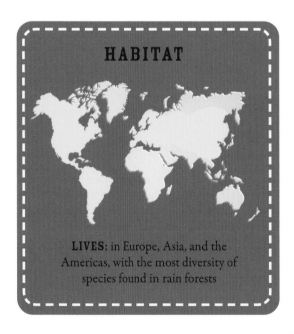

Sticky pads on an assassin bug's front legs help it keep a firm grip on its prey.

HABITAT

LIVES: in Europe, Asia, and the Americas, with the most diversity of species found in rain forests

DID YOU KNOW ... ?

❓ There are about 7,000 species of assassin bug worldwide. They have varying shapes, and their colors range from black and brown to brightly colored.

❓ Deadly assassin bugs are not entirely safe from attack themselves. Predators include birds, spiders, praying mantises, and other assassin bugs.

❓ One species is called the kissing bug because it bites humans around the mouth and will suck blood.

BRILLIANT EATER!

FORMOSAN SUBTERRANEAN TERMITE   *Coptotermes formosanus*

– – – ◆ – – –

These wood chompers live in their millions in enormous underground colonies. They typically nest in the ground and can burrow as deep as 328 feet a day! One colony can eat up to 14 ounces of wood in 24 hours, and can destroy the structure of a building in three months. A colony contains three types of Formosan subterranean termite: reproductives, soldiers, and workers. Reproductives swarm in huge numbers in late spring or summer, usually on humid evenings. When they find a suitable site for a new colony, they break off their wings and look for a mate.

 SIZE: 0.5 inches long

 FOOD: wood, paper, and cardboard

 LIFESPAN: up to 5 years (workers and soldiers), up to 15 years (queen)

 CONSERVATION STATUS: not threatened

 DANGER LEVEL: high—the most dangerous of all underground termites, they eat almost anything

*The Formosan super termites' nest is a network
of underground tunnels and chambers.*

HABITAT

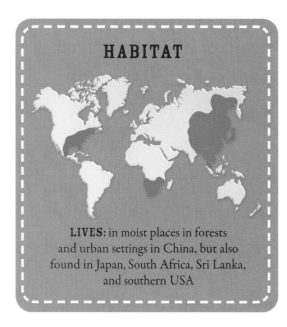

LIVES: in moist places in forests
and urban settings in China, but also
found in Japan, South Africa, Sri Lanka,
and southern USA

DID YOU KNOW ...?

❓ To build their nest, worker termites
combine soil with chewed wood, and glue it
together with saliva and feces. Termite eggs
need temperatures over 68°F (20°C) to hatch.

❓ A queen termite may lay around 2,000 eggs
during her lifetime.

❓ About 15 percent of the colony is made up
of soldiers, significantly more than most other
species. To ward off invaders, soldiers release
a substance called naphthalene, the same
chemical used to make mothballs.

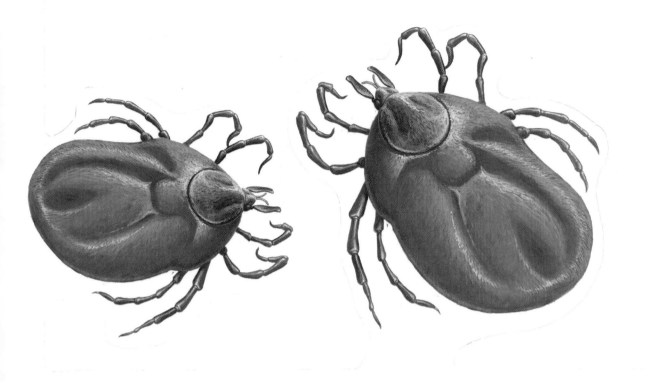

BLOOD SUCKER!

DEER TICK *Ixodes scapularis*

— ◆ — — — —

The tiny deer tick, or black-legged tick, is the size of a sesame seed. It can't jump, fly, or swim. Instead deer ticks crawl to the top of grass or a low-lying shrub and wait for a human or animal to pass. When a host appears, these hungry little ticks climb on board without being noticed. Once the ticks detect their host's body heat and find a quiet, comfortable feeding spot, they stab the skin, embed their sawlike mouthparts in their host and gorge on blood for up to seven days before dropping to the ground. Ticks mate while on their host, but the male tick dies soon after mating.

 SIZE: 0.03–0.1 inches long

 FOOD: the blood of birds, white-tailed deer, and other small mammals

 LIFESPAN: 2–3 years

 CONSERVATION STATUS: not threatened

 DANGER LEVEL: moderate—they can spread diseases if they puncture your skin

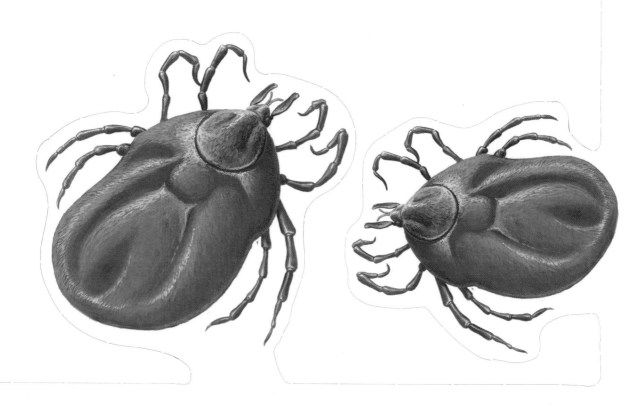

Female deer ticks have a black head and a dark red abdomen. The male ticks are entirely black or dark brown. Both sexes have eight black legs.

HABITAT

LIVES: in North America, southeastern Canada, and northern Mexico

DID YOU KNOW ...?

❓ There are four stages in the life cycle of a tick. The first stage is the egg, the second stage is the six-legged larva, the third is the eight-legged nymph, and the fourth is the adult tick.

❓ After an egg hatches, the tick needs to feed from a different host at each stage of its life cycle in order to survive.

❓ Adult female ticks feed on deer for five to seven days. Adult male ticks rarely feed. Both can survive a whole year without any food!

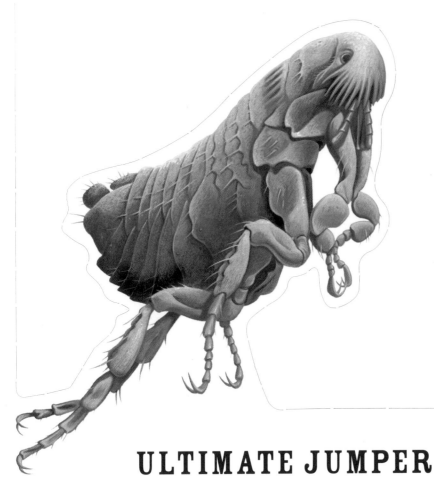

ULTIMATE JUMPER

FLEA *Ctenocephalides*

I t is estimated that there are more than 2,500 flea species living in the world today, with new ones being discovered all the time. Fleas don't have wings, so they can't fly, but they are the world's greatest jumpers. They can leap up to 12 inches forward or seven inches upward, which is more than 100 times their height, and is like a human achieving a 984 foot-long jump. Fleas are also strong and can pull up to 160,000 times their own weight—that's like a human pulling 2,600 double-decker buses! These incredible insects thrive in humid climates.

 SIZE: 0.03–0.1 inches long

 FOOD: blood

 LIFESPAN: 18 months (2–4 as adults)

 CONSERVATION STATUS:
not threatened

 DANGER LEVEL: moderate—
flea bites can make your skin itch
and spread diseases

The flea's champion jumping skills are vital to its survival. It has to leap onto its host so it can feast on blood and reproduce.

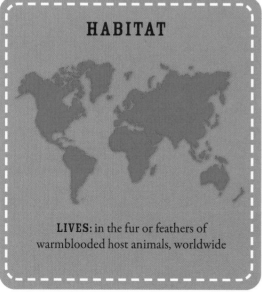

HABITAT

LIVES: in the fur or feathers of warmblooded host animals, worldwide

DID YOU KNOW . . . ?

❓ A jumping flea accelerates 20 times faster than a rocket launching into space.

❓ Giant fleas up to 8 inches long plagued the dinosaurs 165 million years ago. They couldn't jump like today's fleas, but their powerful mouthparts could pierce through tough dinosaur skin.

❓ Female fleas drink the equivalent of 15 times their body weight in blood each day. Like the males, they poop out any excess blood for their larvae to feed on.

STING IN THE TAIL

Deathstalker scorpion *Leiurus quinquestriatus*

⸻ ◆ ⸻

As their alternative name, the Palestinian yellow scorpion, indicates, Deathstalkers are yellow in color, which helps camouflage them in the desert. During the day, they burrow underground or rest under rocks to keep cool. These deadly hunters also lurk under stones at night to wait for passing prey. Their sensitive hairy legs pick up vibrations that alert them to tasty meals nearby. As they pounce, they grip and crush their victim with clawlike pincers and then stab it with a venomous stinger. The poison they release can cause paralysis and death within minutes.

 SIZE: up to 3 inches long

 FOOD: insects, including spiders, worms and other scorpions

 LIFESPAN: 2–6 years

 CONSERVATION STATUS: not threatened

 DANGER LEVEL: high—the toxic venom in their stings make these the most deadly scorpions on Earth

The deathstalker is small compared to other species of scorpion and its pincers are not very strong, so it has to deliver its deadly sting fast.

HABITAT

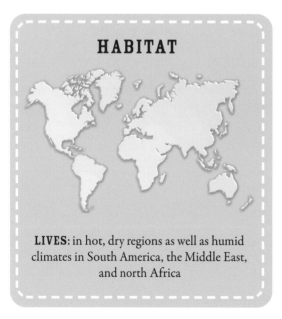

LIVES: in hot, dry regions as well as humid climates in South America, the Middle East, and north Africa

DID YOU KNOW ...?

❓ Some people like to eat scorpions, believing that they improve health and increase strength.

❓ A female can give birth to 100 live scorplings at a time, although 20 to 30 is more common. The newborns climb onto their mother's back, where they live for a few weeks while they're vulnerable to predators.

❓ This scorpion's predators include centipedes and other scorpions, including members of its own species!

UNDERWATER KILLER!

GIANT WATER BUG *Lethocerus*

◆

Worldwide, there are around 160 species of this large, brown, flat-bodied bug. It is active all year round, but particularly during the summer months. The female lays her eggs on aquatic plants, and then the male guards them until they hatch. The giant water bug seems fearless when it comes to hunting, often attacking prey far bigger than itself. It grasps its enemy between two sturdy, long forelegs and swiftly injects it with powerful saliva that turns the poor victim's insides to mush. The giant bug then enjoys lapping up the sludgy remains . . . yuck!

 SIZE: 1.7–3.5 inches long

 FOOD: frogs, salamanders, tadpoles, small fish, and insects

 LIFESPAN: 1–2 years

 CONSERVATION STATUS: not threatened

 DANGER LEVEL: low—this bug can give a painful bite, but it isn't dangerous

A giant water bug will happily attack a frog twice its own size by clutching it in its powerful forelimbs. They've even been known to kill garter snakes and baby turtles!

HABITAT

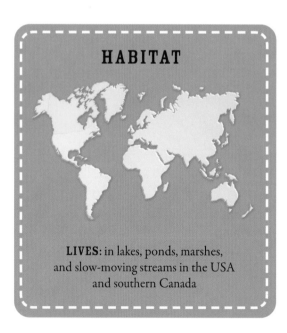

LIVES: in lakes, ponds, marshes, and slow-moving streams in the USA and southern Canada

DID YOU KNOW ...?

❓ To breathe underwater, these bugs use a special snorkel-like tube that extends from their rear to the surface of the water. When this tube is not needed, it withdraws up into the water bug's abdomen.

❓ If in danger, a water bug may play dead. But these bugs can give a painful bite, particularly females protecting their eggs.

❓ The giant water bug has several nicknames, including alligator tick, electric-light bug, and toe biter!

BLOOD-SUCKING BUG

MOSQUITO *Culicidae*

- - - ◆ - - -

Mozzies, drill bugs, skeeters . . . whatever your name for these tiny bloodsucking flies, there's no doubt they're the deadliest critters on Earth because of the number of nasty diseases they spread. There are more than 3,000 species worldwide, but just a few hundred of these are bloodsuckers. It's only the females that drink blood, and this is because they need the extra energy for laying their eggs. A mosquito bite causes an irritating itch, but it's the diseases they can carry—such as malaria, yellow fever, and dengue fever—that are far more serious.

 SIZE: 0.2–0.5 inches long

 FOOD: nectar, blood

 LIFESPAN: female up to 56 days; male 10 days

 CONSERVATION STATUS: not threatened

 DANGER LEVEL: very high—this biter spreads deadly diseases to millions of people every year

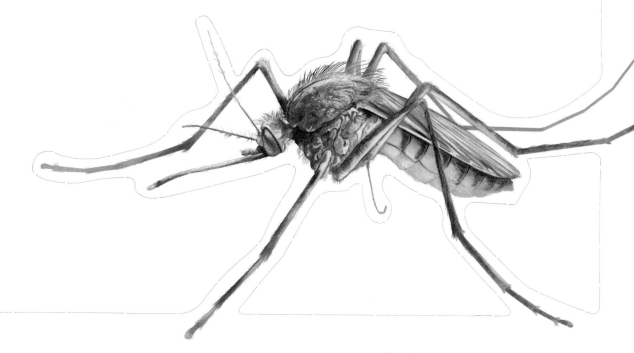

A female mosquito can suck up three times her own body weight during one blood meal.

HABITAT

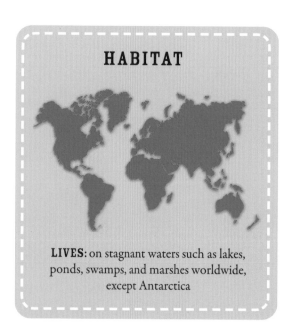

LIVES: on stagnant waters such as lakes, ponds, swamps, and marshes worldwide, except Antarctica

DID YOU KNOW ... ?

❓ Mosquito means "little fly" in Spanish. For all their buzzing, they only reach a maximum flying speed of 1.5 miles (2.4km) per hour.

❓ Mosquitoes love carbon dioxide and can detect it on human breath, which is how they sniff out a meal.

❓ The females lay batches of 50 to 300 eggs on the surface of still water. These batches are called rafts.

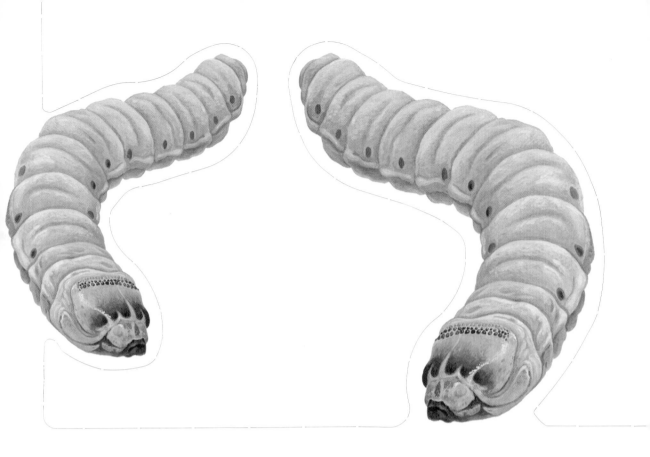

TASTY DINNER!

WITCHETTY GRUB   *Endoxyla leucomochla*

— — — ◆ — — —

These are the chubby, white caterpillars of the cossid moth, which is native to Australia. The grubs feed on the roots of the witchetty bush, and they live alone in underground tunnels that they make in the roots of this bush. They stay in these tunnels until they are ready to emerge and live their brief life as a moth. Witchetty grubs are a traditional food source for indigenous Australians because they are high in protein. Eaten raw or cooked, they're said to have a nutty flavor. When cooked, their skin becomes crispy, like roast chicken.

SIZE: about 4.7 inches long, 1 inches wide

FOOD: witchetty bush roots and sap

LIFESPAN: 2 years (caterpillar), about 2 weeks (moth)

CONSERVATION STATUS: not threatened

DANGER LEVEL: none

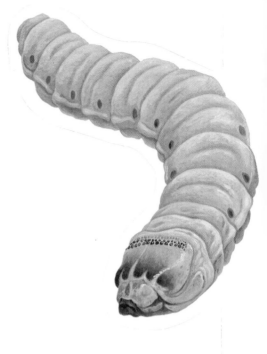

The witchetty grub has a chunky, white body and a brown head.

HABITAT

LIVES: in deep burrows all over Australia, except Tasmania

DID YOU KNOW ... ?

❓ The word *witchetty* comes from a native Australian language, and the grub is traditional Aboriginal Australian food.

❓ The grub has a powerful set of jaws that it uses to tunnel through the roots of the witchetty bush to make its home.

❓ Aboriginal Australian people also use witchetty grubs to make a soothing balm for treating burns and wounds. They grind the grubs into a paste and apply it to damaged skin.

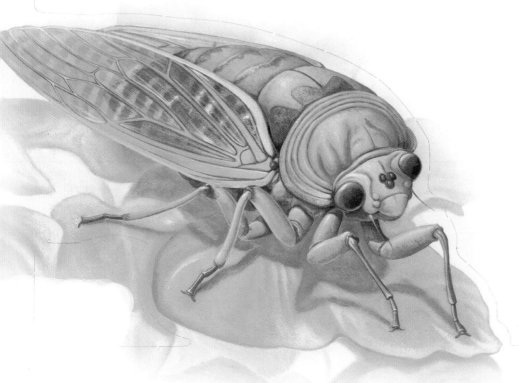

DEAFENING SINGER

NORTHERN GREENGROCER CICADA *Cyclochila virens*

– – – – ◆ – – – –

This noisy flying insect has a large, colorful body, transparent wings, and bulging compound eyes. It's native to Australia and often lives high up in the rain forest canopies. Cicadas are renowned for their screeching song, and this piercingly loud hum is the male's way of attracting a female mate. The singing, which lasts about 20 minutes, usually occurs at dusk but can sometimes be heard on warm, sunny mornings. By grouping together, the cicadas make more noise and scare off any lurking predatory birds.

SIZE: up to 3 inch-long body, up to 2.2 inch forewings

FOOD: tree sap

LIFESPAN: up to 7 years (nymphs), about 6 weeks (adults)

CONSERVATION STATUS: not threatened

DANGER LEVEL: low

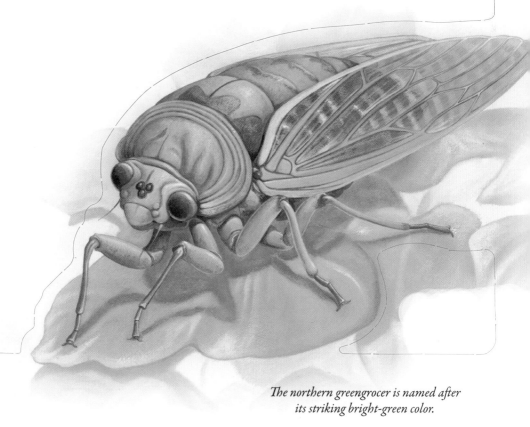

The northern greengrocer is named after its striking bright-green color.

HABITAT

 LIVES: in woodland, rain forests and urban areas in northeastern Queensland, Australia (adult cicadas populate forest canopies)

DID YOU KNOW ... ?

❓ The female cicada lays tiny eggs, which look like grains of rice, inside plant stems.

❓ Cicada eggs hatch about four months after being laid. The hatchlings are called nymphs and live in burrows in the soil, feeding from the sap of plant roots for up to seven years before emerging as adults.

❓ Male greengrocer cicadas tend to come together to sing. Their combined noise level can reach over 120 decibels—that's as loud as a rock concert or a jet engine!

SWEET FOOD STORER

HONEYPOT ANT *Myrmecocystus, Camponotus* and others

There are more than 30 species of honeypot ant living in deserts around the world. They get their name from the worker ants (called repletes) that are fed to bursting during the rainy season. Once their bellies have swollen to the size of a grape with sweet liquid, they hang from the walls inside their nest and wait patiently. When a worker ant needs an energy boost, it nudges a replete with its antennae, signaling for the replete to spit out some honey. The worker will then either suck up the sweet liquid for itself, or carry it off to another ant in need.

SIZE: up to 0.1 inches long

FOOD: the nectar of desert flowers and small insects

LIFESPAN: unknown

CONSERVATION STATUS: not threatened

DANGER LEVEL: none

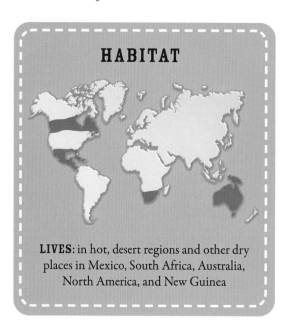

The honeypot ants' sugary liquid stores are vital to the survival of the colony during the dry season, when food and water are scarce.

HABITAT

LIVES: in hot, desert regions and other dry places in Mexico, South Africa, Australia, North America, and New Guinea

DID YOU KNOW ...?

❓ A mature honeypot ant colony may contain up to 15,000 worker ants and one queen that can live up to 11 years, laying around 1,000 eggs per day!

❓ Some species attack each other's colonies. They murder the queen and kidnap the workers to use as slaves.

❓ Some honeypot ants can change color. This may be the result of the type of liquid they store.

NIGHT LIGHT!

FIREFLY *Lampyridae*

The firefly, or lightning bug, is actually a type of winged beetle. Worldwide, there are more than 2,000 species of this glowing nighttime bug. Many species have special light producing organs at the tip of their abdomens, and each species switches its lights on and off following a unique pattern. They use these special flashing patterns to attract a mate. The flashes may also help to keep enemies away by warning them of the firefly's bitter taste. Some species even coordinate their flash patterns so that you can see waves of light moving through groups of fireflies!

SIZE: 0.19–1 inches long

FOOD: mainly nectar and pollen; some species eat smaller fireflies and some don't eat at all

LIFESPAN: about 2 months

CONSERVATION STATUS: not threatened

DANGER LEVEL: moderate—but only if you or your pets eat them

The firefly has a flat dark-brown or black body and the back of its head is red, pink, or orange.

HABITAT

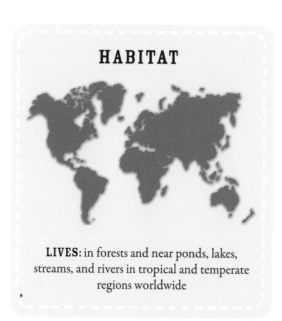

LIVES: in forests and near ponds, lakes, streams, and rivers in tropical and temperate regions worldwide

DID YOU KNOW...?

❓ Around the world people have many different names for fireflies, including glow flies, moon bugs, firefly beetles, golden sparklers, big dippers, and fire devils. Firefly larvae are often called glow worms.

❓ The female lays her eggs underground for protection—even firefly eggs glow!

❓ When the larvae hatch, they remain underground until adulthood, feeding on slugs, snails, and worms.

LONG, LEGGY & LETHAL!

GIANT CENTIPEDE *Scolopendra gigantea*

◆

The speedy giant centipede, also known as the Peruvian giant yellow-leg centipede or Amazonian giant centipede, can grow up to 12 inches long and 1 inch wide. Its body is made up of 21 to 23 flattened segments, each with a pair of legs attached to it. The "legs" on the first body segment are actually a pair of deadly, venomous fangs, which the centipede uses to snatch and kill prey. Its eyesight is very poor, so it relies heavily on touch and chemoreceptors (sense organs that react to chemicals) when it moves around and hunts for food.

 SIZE: up to 12 inches long

 FOOD: crickets, worms, snails, lizards, toads, and mice

 LIFESPAN: about 10 years

 CONSERVATION STATUS: not threatened

 DANGER LEVEL: moderate—it gives a painful, poisonous bite that can make you feel sick for days

The meat-eating giant centipede uses its antennae to detect bats, which it hunts in the dark caves of South America.

HABITAT

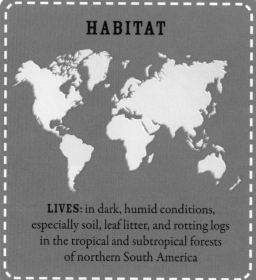

LIVES: in dark, humid conditions, especially soil, leaf litter, and rotting logs in the tropical and subtropical forests of northern South America

DID YOU KNOW...?

❓ The poison contained in a giant centipede bite can seriously wound but is rarely deadly to humans.

❓ When attacking prey, the giant centipede wraps its body around its victim, injects it with poison, then chops it into pieces to gobble up.

❓ The centipede hunts for bats by hanging on a cave wall by its back legs, then swinging out and grabbing hold of one as it swoops past.